WHO'S IN CHARGE?

WHO'S IN CHARGE?

SYSTEMS OF POWER:
CHINA

Katie Dicker

Franklin Watts
First published in Great Britain in 2020 by The Watts Publishing Group
Copyright © The Watts Publishing Group, 2020

Produced for Franklin Watts by
White-Thomson Publishing Ltd
www.wtpub.co.uk

ISBN: 978 1 4451 6919 4 (hb) 978 1 4451 6920 0 (pb)

Credits
Editor: Katie Dicker
Designer: Dan Prescott, Couper Street Type Co.
Consultant: Philip Parker
Illustrations: Techtype (4t, 35b, 43)

The publisher would like to thank the following for permission to reproduce their pictures: Alamy: Witold Skrypczak 6, Sally and Richard Greenhill 7t, Xinhua 20, 24 and 42, Newscom 25; Getty: Apic/Contributor cover l, Wally McNamee/CORBIS cover m, swim ink 2 llc/Contributor 9t, GOH CHAI HIN/AFP 12, STR/AFP 16r, Joel Carillet 26, Laszlo Mates 33t, matejmo 38, real444 45b; Shutterstock: 360b cover r and 16l, Nithid 4bl, Jiraphoto 4bm, Clkraus 4br, Aphotostory 5, Everett Historical 7m, axz700 9b, Canadapanda 11, gyn9037 13t, Eastimages 13b, TonyV3112 14, XiXinXing 15t, Sean Pavone 15b, Frederic Legrand – COMEO 17, Belish 18, photocosmos1 19t, aradaphotography 19b, Hung Chung Chih 21, Maridav 22t, LuckyStep 22b, Casimiro PT 23t, Lemberg Vector studio 23bl, 23bm and 23br, Liudmila Kotvitckaia 27t, LO Kin-hei 27b, testing 28 and 40, Gil Corzo 29, humphery 30t, Arthimedes 30b, anek.soowannaphoom 31, Alexander Ryabintsev 32, plavevski 33b, SL Chen 35t, M-SUR 36, Alejo Miranda 37t, Peter Stein 37b, Sheila Fitzgerald 39, L.F 41t, ArtisticPhoto 41b, Nick Poon 44, SvedOliver 45t; Wikimedia: William Elliott Debenham 7b, Schumacher, Karl H. 10; IMF/MGM Research: reference for 34.

All design elements from Shutterstock.

Printed in Malaysia

Franklin Watts
An imprint of
Hachette Children's Group
Part of The Watts Publishing Group
Carmelite House
50 Victoria Embankment
London EC4Y 0DZ

An Hachette UK Company
www.hachette.co.uk
www.franklinwatts.co.uk

MIX
Paper from
responsible sources
FSC
www.fsc.org FSC® C104740

CONTENTS

WHAT makes China unique?   4

WHAT is communism?   6

HOW did China's communism change?   8

WHAT are today's key challenges?   14

WHO is Xi Jinping?   16

WHO is Li Keqiang?   18

WHAT is a one-party state?   20

WHAT about human rights?   26

HOW does the government work?   28

WHY is the army important?   32

WHAT about the economy?   34

WHAT influence does China have?   36

WHAT about global influences?   38

HOW does Xi Jinping want to govern?   42

WHAT lies ahead?   44

Glossary   46

Further information   47

Index   48

Can you imagine governing over 1.4 billion people? About a fifth of the world's population live in China, and the decisions of their government affect their education, their job opportunities, their healthcare and the welfare of their families. What happens in China has an impact on the rest of the world, too.

HUGE NATION

China is the world's fourth largest country (after Russia, Canada and the USA), and has the biggest population. Its citizens have a strong identity, given that most (92 per cent) are Han Chinese – the world's largest ethnic group. China also has the world's longest international land border (22,147 km). Governing a nation of this size and protecting its borders is a real challenge.

★ China borders 14 other nations. Most people live on the east coast. The mountainous west and rural interior are more sparsely populated.

Leabharlanna Fhine Gall

★ China has a varied climate – from the Gobi Desert (north) to lush rice paddies (south and centre) and the snowy peaks of Mount Everest (southwest border).

FALL FROM GRACE

China boasts the world's longest continuous civilisation. For over 4,000 years, China was governed by ruling dynasties and a succession of emperors. But a 'Century of Humiliation' (1839–1949) saw foreign invasions from Britain, France, Germany, Japan, Russia and the USA. China lost control of a third of its territory and the nation perceived it had lost its dignity. China had fallen from grace.

'China? There lies a sleeping giant. Let him sleep! For when he wakes he will move the world.'

Attributed to Napoléon Bonaparte, French military leader, c.1803

CHANGING TIMES

Yet time is a healer. Over recent decades, modernisation and industrialisation have helped the country to regain its pride and prestige. Since 1949, China's rule has been shaped around a system of government called communism. The 'Century of Humiliation' will never be forgotten, but many believe this new style of government overcomes past vulnerabilities.

RISING WEALTH

China's vast population brings a huge workforce and the country is rich in natural resources. Rapid economic growth has seen China become the world's second largest economy (after the USA). China's new status also gives it a greater voice on the global stage. Can China sustain its development? Will the international balance of power shift? Who's really in charge of global politics these days? As China embarks on a new era of dominance, the world waits with anticipation.

★ China's 'Great Wall' was built from the seventh century BCE, to defend the historical northern border. Surviving parts are about 500 years old.

WHAT IS COMMUNISM?

For thousands of years, people have argued about the best ways to govern and how to resolve the problems of inequality within societies. The ancient Greeks discussed political philosophy in the sixth century BCE, and different styles of leadership began to emerge. In the late nineteenth century, a new political system called communism developed in Russia and spread to other nations, too.

EQUAL SOCIETY

Communism aims to create a society where everything is shared equally. Instead of individuals competing for gain, everyone works together for the same reward. There are no individuals employing workers in their factories or farms – the government owns and controls these 'means of production'. The aim of true communism is to create a classless society with no distinctions of wealth. This is the opposite of 'capitalism', where private ownership and competition create a gap between rich and poor.

★ This communist poster is shown in a Latvian museum. The hammer and sickle represent industrial workers and peasants uniting to build a communist society.

REALITY BITES

Communism sounds kind and compassionate, but is there a catch? History has shown that no large society can achieve pure communism. In a true communist society, the community makes decisions, but to keep large societies under control, a small group of people inevitably takes charge. Instead of everyone being equal, a government has to make important decisions on their behalf. Citizens may be well cared for, but they have less freedom and control over their daily lives. People have to give up their land or livestock, education is tailored to the needs of the state, religious views are suppressed and jobs are dictated by what's required.

★ In a communist society, the community works together and profits are shared equally.

★ KARL MARX AND FRIEDRICH ENGELS

Communism is a political system based on the ideas of two German philosophers – Karl Marx (1818–1883) and Friedrich Engels (1820–1895). Their theory, known as Marxism, can be summarised by Marx's phrase 'From each according to his ability, to each according to his needs'. In Marxism, people contribute their skills for the good of all and everyone's welfare is taken care of. Cooperation replaces competition, helping to bridge the gap between rich and poor.

Karl Marx

Friedrich Engels

HOW DID CHINA'S COMMUNISM CHANGE?

In 1912, the last emperor of China's Qing dynasty abdicated and revolutionaries established the 'Republic of China'. The country became divided, however, when local military leaders (warlords) vied for control. In the turmoil, two major political parties established themselves – the Kuomintang (KMT) and the Communist Party of China (CPC). After a bitter civil war between them, communism came to China.

'Political power grows out of the barrel of a gun.'

Mao Zedong during the Chinese Civil War, 1927

BATTLE FOR POWER

Under the leadership of Chiang Kai-shek, the KMT suppressed rivals (both warlords and communists) in a civil war, to begin a period of rule from 1928. But during the fighting, Japan invaded the disputed region of Manchuria, and later China itself (1937–45). Some thought the KMT had failed to protect China, and gravitated towards communist ideas. Communism also gained supporters in the countryside.

COMMUNIST VICTORY

The Chinese Civil War resumed after the Second World War (1939–45), when a stronger communist side emerged victorious. The KMT retreated to Taiwan, establishing the Republic of China on the island in 1949, while the mainland was renamed the People's Republic of China under Mao Zedong's CPC. From 1953, a five-year plan saw industrialisation with heavy industry, but later China's communism (known as 'Maoism') began to shift its focus to farming. China was a largely agricultural society, so farmers (rather than factory workers) were key.

紧跟毛主席在大风大浪中前进

Mao ruled like a dictator, but a 'cult of personality' overcame his limitations. He is still greatly revered in China today.

CATCHING UP

After decades of war, China had fallen behind the Western world. To catch up, Mao launched the Great Leap Forward (1958–61) favouring manpower over machines. Property and land were redistributed and communal kitchens left women free to work. Villages ran small steel furnaces, but competing demands took workers away from the fields and bad weather caused a terrible famine. Around 30 million people died. Mao retreated while some in the CPC considered moving away from communism altogether.

REGAINING CONTROL

To regain control and reassert communist values, Mao launched the Cultural Revolution (1966–76). Colleges were closed and students encouraged to join the 'Red Guards', to harass intellectuals and the middle classes and to inform on 'non-believers', who were severely punished or sent to labour camps. It is thought that up to two million people lost their lives. Cultural influences, such as art and literature, were also destroyed. Mao had brought the 'Century of Humiliation' to a close, but with a crippled economy and divided nation, people began to lose faith in the government. Something new was needed.

CHANGE OF TACK

After Mao's death in 1976, a power struggle saw Deng Xiaoping emerge victorious and the government moved away from Maoism. Deng's communism became known as 'socialism with Chinese characteristics'. Instead of a classless society, citizens worked in a variety of jobs towards the greater good. China was far behind the West in terms of income and technology, and needed a new path.

PARTY REFORMS

Initial reforms within the CPC brought fixed terms of office and a retirement age to keep 'new blood' coming through the ranks. Government bodies were revised to move power away from the centre and prevent dictatorial rule. Deng's government gave citizens greater freedom, but the CPC still held huge sway in some areas. For example, a new one-child policy controlled the growing population (see page 15).

In 1978, the USA became China's largest trading partner. Deng was the first Chinese leader to visit the USA, seen here with President Jimmy Carter in 1979.

RISING ECONOMY

Deng also prioritised the economy. A focus on agriculture sustained food supplies, and citizens could work in their speciality (instead of working as a group on a collective farm), making the economy more productive. Young people were encouraged to study again and intellectuals regained their status. Deng's 'Four Modernisations' (see page 11) needed capital so he invited US and European investment. Relations improved with Japan and the Soviet Union, too.

THE FOUR MODERNISATIONS

Agriculture – machines increase food production and land returned to farming families. Some harvest sold to government, but remainder sold for profit, encouraging farmers to grow more.

Industry – shift from heavy to light industry sees a rise in export of cheap goods. Factory managers choose products and keep excess profits. China becomes a global producer of steel, iron, oil and coal.

Science and technology – four Special Economic Zones (SEZs) attract foreign companies, bringing a flow of technology ideas to China. New focus on maths and science in schools.

Defence – weapons modernised and soldiers trained in modern tactics/ techniques. More soldiers sign up.

CRUSHING OPPOSITION

For many, however, economic prosperity wasn't enough without the freedom to enjoy it. Growing inflation and corruption caused resentment, too. By 1989, mass demonstrations reflected the anti-communist revolutions that were taking place in Europe at the same time. Tiananmen Square in Beijing was a particular hotspot. Undecided how to react, the government almost collapsed with internal divisions. On the night of 3–4 June, however, Deng ordered the army to intervene and hundreds of demonstrators were killed. Deng's actions were condemned worldwide and he resigned his official posts, but he remained influential until his death in 1997.

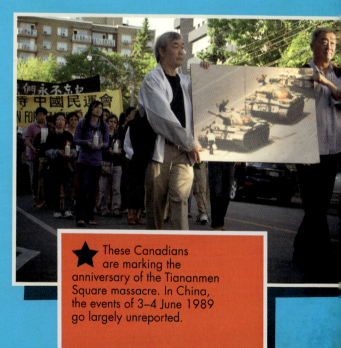

★ These Canadians are marking the anniversary of the Tiananmen Square massacre. In China, the events of 3–4 June 1989 go largely unreported.

LEARNING FROM MISTAKES

The CPC blamed the civil unrest in Tiananmen Square on excessive decentralisation. They tightened the Party's control and fused leadership at the top (president, general secretary, and chairman of the Central Military Commission). To prevent another uprising, however, they needed to give greater social and political freedom to China's citizens.

PEACEFUL SUCCESSIONS

In 1993, Deng Xiaoping aided the appointment of Jiang Zemin as China's president. When Jiang voluntarily retired from his position a decade later, it was the first time a leader of the CPC had left office without dying or being deposed. His successor, Hu Jintao, also served for a decade (2003–13).

'After 100 years of struggle, China has stood up again as a giant.'

Jiang Zemin, state visit to the USA, 1997

JIANG ZEMIN

Former mayor of Shanghai, Jiang Zemin continued to strengthen the economy while keeping a tight grip on political power. Jiang closed unprofitable state-sector enterprises, encouraged private firms to flourish and continued to invest in the military. Under his watch, foreign relations also improved – in 1997, Hong Kong reverted to Chinese rule for example (see page 30) and a state visit to the USA brought a surge in US-China trade. Exports also rose rapidly when China joined the World Trade Organization in 2001.

★ Under Jiang Zemin (right) and Hu Jintao (left), a strong central government brought economic growth, improved welfare provision and greater national prestige.

HU JINTAO

In 2003, China was the world's sixth largest economy and fourth largest exporter. By the end of Hu Jintao's rule, China was second and first respectively. As China's markets opened to foreign trade, many high-tech companies, such as Apple, moved their manufacturing to China, attracted by the cheap labour, fast production and small supply chain (using Chinese components and selling to China's fast-growing consumer market). Investments in travel (air, road and rail) helped to bridge the development gap between China's urban coast and rural interior. Some analysts claim the middle class in rural China grew from 3 per cent in 1988 to 53 per cent in 2007.

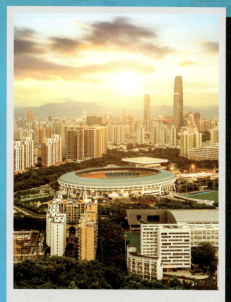

Special Economic Zones in cities such as Shenzhen (above) helped China overtake the UK, France, Germany and Japan to become the world's second largest economy in 2010.

BEIJING OLYMPICS

The 2008 Beijing Olympics were an opportunity for China to show the world what it was made of – and were a monumental success. At a cost of around US$45 billion – including a new airport terminal, high-speed rail network and environmental measures – they were among the most expensive Games held.

★ The design of Beijing's 2008 Olympic stadium (the 'Bird's Nest') was a symbol of China's rising wealth and world status.

WHAT ARE TODAY'S KEY CHALLENGES?

The rule of Jiang Zemin and Hu Jintao brought increased prosperity to China, but an open market created huge gaps between rich and poor. Growing corruption within the CPC also brought the risk of civil unrest. When Xi Jinping took over in 2013, those seeking political and economic reform welcomed his strong leadership style and desire for change.

GROWING DISPARITY

China's rapid industrialisation has caused environmental degradation (see page 40). Can China reduce its pollution without disrupting the economy? Urban migration has widened the gap between rich urban areas and poor rural regions. With fewer people working the land, can China maintain its food supply? China's growing urban middle class also demand better wages and welfare, making it more difficult for China to maintain its competitiveness.

CHANGING DEMOGRAPHIC

According to the Chinese Academy of Social Sciences, China's population could peak at 1.44 billion in 2029. The challenge for the next decade is to create enough jobs (and food) for this population. But due to China's one-child policy (see page 15), the population will then begin to decline and age. A reduced workforce and lower consumer spending will also slow economic growth.

★ By 2050, around a third of China's population will be over 60, putting a strain on welfare provisions.

Due to China's one-child policy, each child now grows up to support two parents and four grandparents, although inherited wealth has grown too.

★ ONE-CHILD POLICY

Mao believed a populous country was a prosperous one – under his rule, China's population nearly doubled. But from 1979, due to increased social, economic and environmental problems, Deng Xiaoping restricted urban families to one child/birth. The policy is believed to have prevented at least 200 million births, but caused longer-term problems. China now has 33 million more men than women, for example (males are considered a better support to parents financially in old age which led to a rise in female infanticide/ abandonment or selective abortions). The policy changed in 2016, but some families still choose to have just one child (see page 44).

FOREIGN AFFAIRS

China lost control of a third of its territory during the 'Century of Humiliation' (see page 5). It has reasserted control over Tibet, Xinjiang and Hong Kong, but Taiwan is still a sticking point. There are also disputed territories in the East and South China Seas (see page 43). Some analysts think China is looking to regain lost lands to restore its former status.

★ In 2015, almost 169 million people in China moved from rural to urban areas, attracted by better-paid work in the cities.

WHO IS XI JINPING?

When Xi Jinping became China's president in 2013, he declared his dream of making China prosperous, powerful and proud again. Xi's father had helped to bring the CPC to power in 1949, and Xi's vision upheld the values of old communist China with a new twist for a modern era (see page 42).

POWERFUL POSITION

Today, Xi Jinping is China's most powerful man. As well as being president, he is general secretary of the CPC, chairman of the Central Military Commission and commander-in-chief of the armed forces. Since he governs the world's largest population and second largest economy, he also has the potential to change lives globally.

This postage stamp commemorated the 100th anniversary of the birth of Xi's father, Xi Zhongxun, a communist war hero.

★ In 2018, *Forbes* magazine named Xi Jinping the world's most powerful person. He replaced Russia's president, Vladimir Putin, who had held the top spot for four years.

FORMATIVE YEARS

Born in 1953, Xi was the second son of Xi Zhongxun, who fought alongside Mao to bring the CPC to power and also served as deputy prime minister. For this reason, Xi Jinping is known as a 'princeling' and his early life was one of privilege. But when Xi was ten, his father fell out of favour with Mao and was imprisoned. As his son, Xi was sent to the countryside for seven years' hard labour. Xi helped villagers to grow crops and build a dam. For a time, he lived in a cave and slept on a straw mat. These formative years made Xi a resilient leader. He later gained a degree in chemical engineering, a degree in Marxist philosophy and a PhD in law.

'Happiness does not fall out of the blue and dreams will not come true by themselves… working hard is the most honourable, noblest, greatest and most beautiful virtue.'

Xi Jinping, talking to exemplary workers at a trade union convention, 2013

RISE TO THE TOP

Xi was desperate to join the CPC, but had to apply ten times before he was accepted in 1974. In the 1980s, he started his regional political career and gradually rose through the ranks. In 2002, he was elected to important CPC committees and in 2007 became Party chief in Shanghai, before joining the Politburo Standing Committee (see page 28). He was promoted to vice-president (2008–13) and vice-chairman of the Central Military Commission (2010–12). Xi had become President Hu Jintao's natural successor by the time he stepped down in 2013.

★ In 1987, Xi married his second wife, Peng Liyuan, an award-winning folk singer. Their daughter Xi Mingze was born in 1992.

WHO IS LI KEQIANG?

Many consider China's second-most powerful person to be Li Keqiang. As premier of the State Council (see page 29), Li is the highest-level government official. Like Hu Jintao before him, Li is also one of the first generation to rise to power through the Communist Youth League (CYL). His strong background in economics is highly regarded.

PRIZE-WINNING STUDENT

Li's father was a local Party official in Anhui province. He offered to train Li for the local Party leadership, but Li wanted to continue with his studies first. He gained a degree in law and a PhD in economics from Peking University. Li's doctoral dissertation was awarded China's highest prize in economics – the Sun Yefang Prize.

POLITICAL RISE

During his student days, Li became the university's CYL secretary and then a member of the national CYL secretariat. In 1983, he married Cheng Hong, whose father was deputy secretary of the CYL Central Committee. From 1993 to 1998, Li served as the CYL's first secretary. He worked closely with Hu Jintao, who also rose through the ranks of the CYL.

★ As head of government, Li is seen as the 'general manager' of the world's second largest economy.

YOUNG GOVERNOR

In 1998, Li became the youngest governor of a province at the time – aged 43, he led Henan province with a population (94 million) bigger than most European countries. Hu Jintao chose Li as his successor, although Li lost out to Xi Jinping. Li was appointed premier of the State Council and is second only to Xi Jinping on the Politburo Standing Committee (see page 28).

ADMINISTRATIVE ROLE

Li organises and administers China's government (overseeing departments and agencies) and announces candidates for key personnel to the country's 'parliament'. In 2018, *Forbes* magazine named Li the world's fifteenth most powerful person, but some consider his power to be mainly administrative.

'The world today needs both Western thinking and Oriental vision.'
Li Keqiang, *Financial Times* article, 2012

★ Li often travels abroad or hosts leaders in China to secure economic deals and partnerships. He is seen here with Germany's chancellor, Angela Merkel.

Forbes magazine rates a person's power on how many people they influence, the financial resources they control and how they use their power to change the world.

LI'S VISION

Li uses economic data to aid government decisions. He favours free trade, action on climate change and improved welfare services. He has focused on moving China towards a consumption-based economy, to be less reliant on exports (see page 34) and favours investment in the military to protect China's security.

ONE-PARTY STATE?

China has been governed by one political party since 1949 – the Communist Party of China (CPC). Although another eight minor political parties exist, they're not allowed to challenge the authority of the CPC. This makes China effectively a one-party state. Other one-party states of the world include North Korea, Cuba and Vietnam.

PARTY MEMBERSHIP

With nearly 90 million members, the CPC is the world's second largest political party (after India's Bharatiya Janata Party). Joining the CPC brings access to information and particular jobs, as well as networking opportunities. Membership is granted after lengthy checks, assessments and training. As a result, the Party is mostly made up of government officials, army officers and employees of state-run companies. It is not representative of China as a whole.

SYMBOLIC ELECTIONS

Without the choice of a ruling party, elections are largely symbolic. Xi Jinping was elected president with a majority of 99.86 per cent from the votes of around 3,000 members of the National People's Congress (NPC – see page 28). China's system of government is a far cry from that of democratic nations, where ordinary citizens vote for the politicians who they want to represent them. In China, for approximately every 460,000 people, just one person got to vote for their new leader.

About 0.0002 per cent of China's population got to vote for their new president in 2013.

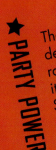
The CPC has a huge influence over people's lives. It decides what Chinese children learn at school; it restricts radio and television programmes and newspaper articles; it has even controlled the number of babies born in China. State-owned media companies are regulated and internet use is monitored and restricted. This helps the CPC to justify its authority and to uphold its popular image.

FIRM GRIP

With a sole political party at the helm, China's government can react quickly when policy changes are needed. The Party also controls the military (which has a duty to uphold the rule of the Party). The role of the CPC within society is shifting slightly (see page 31), but challenges to the Party's rule are still swiftly dealt with. The CPC has a country to govern and intends to stay in control.

★ Soldiers on patrol in Beijing. With control of the military, the CPC can withstand any threat to its authority.

GROWING TREND

Over 800 million people in China are now online, although their use of the internet is tightly controlled. With internet use growing rapidly (an estimated 50 million new Chinese users got online in 2018), the government is under increased pressure to control online content.

DOUBLE-EDGED SWORD

In 2013, the CPC's Central Committee described the internet as a 'double-edged sword' with 'positive energy and negative energy... coexisting side by side.' The internet is crucial for China's economic development, but the CPC wants to stay in control.

★ In China, 58 per cent of the population is now online, with 98 per cent of those using smartphones.

REGAINING POWER

Under Hu Jintao's regime, a little more freedom was found online. Political bloggers gained followers and people used virtual private networks (VPNs) to access blocked websites. Things changed after the Arab Spring of 2011 however, when the internet helped to spark revolutions across the Middle East. When Xi Jinping took office, he vowed to take a firmer stand.

★ The CPC prevents the sharing of online content that might be harmful to the state, or to the Party's popular image.

STRICT CONTROLS

China's 'great firewall' allows the government to monitor data and block internet traffic to and from the country. New laws determine acceptable internet use, VPNs have been blocked and chat-room administrators are held accountable for published material. More recently, an online tool called the 'great cannon' can change or replace website content. At least two million people (as well as volunteers) are employed to monitor and censor online content. The government also encourages users to censor each other and report suspicious activity.

★ These popular social media apps are used in China, but are closely monitored and controlled by the government.

★ MONITORING SOCIAL MEDIA

The CPC has replaced social media apps with their own government-controlled versions. Instead of WhatsApp, messages sent via 'WeChat' are shared with the government. Videos uploaded to 'Youku' are closely monitored and anything that could be seen as dissident is taken down. Likewise, the CPC has a hold over replacements for Twitter (Weibo), Google (Baidu) and Facebook Messenger (QQ). Social media forums are flooded with positive comments about the CPC.

CORRUPTION AT THE TOP

With just one party at the helm, corruption can creep into government decisions. Growing prosperity and the centralised control of resources can lead to bribery or inappropriate use of funds. There is evidence that some government officials in the past have also favoured family and friends when making appointments.

RISKY BUSINESS

Corruption can undermine economic development, inflating costs and creating inefficiency (without competition). Some corrupt practices ignore human rights, health and safety and environmental or building regulations. When a government is unable to justify its actions, people lose faith and civil unrest can brew.

★ A meeting of China's Central Commission for Discipline Inspection – working to maintain the CPC's reputation and to stamp out inefficiency.

REGAINING REPUTATION

In 2012, Bo Xilai – a former Party chief and Politburo member (see page 28) – was linked to the murder of a British businessman and later charged with corruption, bribery and abuse of power. He was expelled from the Party and given a life sentence in prison. When Xi Jinping came to power, he was determined to restore the CPC's reputation.

TIGERS AND FLIES

Xi carried out a massive anti-corruption drive, known as the 'tigers and flies' campaign. Anti-corruption bodies were strengthened, and the Central Commission for Discipline Inspection punished around 1.5 million CPC members for corruption, bad management or breaking with the party line. Xi's zealous approach left no stone unturned. He wanted to restore public respect for the Party, though some commentators claim it was also a way to purge political rivals and enforce absolute loyalty. Xi has also been careful with his own public image. He avoids lavish banquets and tries to travel by modest means.

ZHOU YONGKANG

In 2015, the most senior CPC official to face corruption charges was given a life sentence for bribery, abuse of power and leaking state secrets. Zhou Yongkang (above) was China's ex-security chief and a Politburo Standing Committee member. His trial showed that no one was above the law. Zhou had a close working relationship with Bo Xilai, and many of his close aides were also investigated or sacked.

WHAT ABOUT HUMAN RIGHTS?

While the CPC has cracked down on anti-Party activities at the top, opposition to the Party has been suppressed within society for decades. The West heavily criticises China for its lack of free expression and human rights violations, which it is claimed span excessive censorship, detaining prisoners without trial and even torture and executions.

TRIAL AND RETRIBUTION

Those accused of breaking the law are arrested and some imprisoned. Their lawyers have also been targeted – with some detained or simply reported missing. Laws have been passed in the interest of 'national security' and human rights groups claim many trials don't meet international standards of law. They say the welfare of the Party appears to come before protection of individual rights.

MINORITY GROUPS

Minority groups have been supported in some areas (the Mongols, for example, were exempt from the one-child policy due to their limited population). Yet China's majority Han Chinese population have the louder voice. In Tibet and Xinjiang, for example, cultural influences are in decline. Local languages have been phased out from schools and Tibet's borders are often closed to prevent protests from the independence movement.

★ A young Tibetan woman protests in the USA against human rights abuses in her homeland. Protests of this kind would not be possible in China.

RELIGIOUS VIEWS

Some religions are officially recognised in China, but others have been repressed for years. Muslims in Xinjiang and spiritual groups such as the Falun Gong, for example, have been persecuted, and followers harassed or imprisoned. Campaigners believe some have even been killed.

KEEPING TABS

China is currently developing a social credit system to monitor the behaviour of individuals and companies, using digital data to rate their trustworthiness. Rewards and punishments are given accordingly, such as restrictions on employment, travel or access to credit. The CPC wants to make integrity a widespread social value, but human rights groups are concerned.

Members of the Falun Gong meditate in Taiwan. The movement has been banned in China since 1999.

Memorial services were held around the world for Liu Xiaobo (pictured) who spent most of his life fighting for freedom, but died in state custody.

★ **LIU XIAOBO**

Some human rights cases have gained worldwide attention. In 2010, Chinese writer and activist Liu Xiaobo was awarded the Nobel Peace Prize while serving an 11-year prison sentence. Liu had declared the internet 'truly God's gift to the Chinese people' and had used it to spread his democratic views, calling for political reform in China. The world was anticipating his release in 2020, but he died from cancer in 2017, aged 61.

GOVERNMENT WORK?

China's system of government has a pyramid structure, with ultimate power at the top flowing down to counties, cities, towns and villages. Power is officially divided in three ways – the Party (CPC), the state and the army. In reality, however, the CPC has complete control of every level of government.

THE POLITBURO

Appointments to the Politburo are announced at the CPC's National Congress held every five years. This group of up to 25 powerful state figures discusses every political decision in China. Ultimate power rests with the Politburo's Standing Committee which currently has seven members. In 2017, Xi Jinping appointed older members to the Standing Committee (see page 29). None is considered his 'successor'. Women are poorly represented – there is currently only one female member of the Politburo, and there has never been a female Standing Committee member.

CHINA'S PARLIAMENT

Loyalty to the Party comes first in the National People's Congress (NPC), for example, since 70 per cent are Party members. The NPC has the power to make laws, change the constitution and elect state officials. It also elects its own Standing Committee to fine-tune policy issues. Some say the NPC is a 'rubber stamp' to justify Party decisions, but it has been known to insist on revisions to draft laws before giving its approval.

★ The NPC meets in the Great Hall of the People in Beijing. Its nearly 3,000 delegates hold office for five years.

STATE COUNCIL

The State Council is in charge of day-to-day procedures. It drafts and manages the national economic plan and the state budget, and is responsible for law and order. Chaired by premier Li Keqiang (see pages 18–19), it contains the head of each governmental department and agency.

CENTRAL MILITARY COMMISSION

The Central Military Commission controls decisions relating to China's military – the People's Liberation Army (PLA, see page 32) – including senior appointments, troop deployment and military spending. Most members are senior generals, although senior leaders of the CPC hold important positions.

★ POLITBURO STANDING COMMITTEE, FROM 2017

Xi Jinping – (see page 16)

Li Keqiang – (see page 18)

Li Zhanshu – Chairman of the NPC Standing Committee

Han Zheng – Executive Vice-Premier of the State Council

Wang Yang – Chairman of the Chinese People's Political Consultative Conference

Wang Huning – Director of the Central Policy Research Office

Zhao Leji – Head of the Central Commission for Discipline Inspection

★ As president, Xi Jinping holds the highest state office. But this formal position has little influence in practice. He holds more real power as general secretary of the CPC.

PARTY ELDERS

Retired leaders are keen to bring their own supporters into government to maintain their influence over a new generation. Party elders want to ensure the popularity and influence of their children too, and can hold great sway. Some party elders, for example, put pressure on Deng Xiaoping to order army intervention in Tiananmen Square (see page 11).

29

LOCAL POLITICS

China's vast size means the CPC must maintain a level of agreement among Party members, local leaders and the general population. China has 22 provinces (23 if Taiwan is included), five autonomous regions populated by a particular ethnic group (see page 4) and two special administrative regions (Hong Kong and Macao) – former European colonies. In 2019, mass protests in Hong Kong demanded the protection of political freedoms, challenging the authority of the CPC.

Local Party members meet to discuss policies and elect local government – as seen here in Jiangxi province.

POWER FLOW

Key decisions are taken at the top and filter down to the regions. Local leaders who fail to carry out policies are punished. At each level, Party and government structures sit side by side but Party representatives take precedence. Party members can vote on local policies and leaders, but once a decision is reached, it must be respected. Party control is looser in autonomous regions to respect particular circumstances and quell unrest. The Party strives to represent the interests of the people, but at the same time dictates what some of these needs are (such as family planning, see page 15).

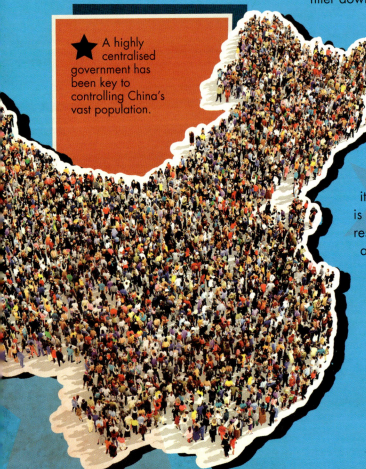

★ A highly centralised government has been key to controlling China's vast population.

RISING THROUGH THE RANKS

There are two major routes to political power in China today – being a princeling (see page 17) or becoming a member of the Communist Youth League (see page 18). Children tend to join the CYL at high school, having learnt about the CPC in their younger years. To advance politically however, they need to gain and retain the support of the people in power. China tries to rule by merit, but in reality political favours are still given.

'[We must always] maintain the Party's flesh-and-blood ties with the masses of the people.'

Xi Jinping, CPC
19th National
Congress, 2017

DIFFERENT INFLUENCES

China's growing wealth has led to speculation that the power of the centre is waning. Party secretaries of large cities such as Beijing and Shanghai, and governors of important provinces such as Sichuan and Guangdong, wield great power, and local tax revenues are vital. Influential businessmen and women have a growing influence, too (see page 35). Analysts still agree, however, that it's safer to stick to the party line for the sake of one's career.

★ The success of cities such as Beijing has an impact on China's social, economic and political development.

WHY IS THE ARMY IMPORTANT?

With a border over 22,000 km long and 14 neighbouring countries, it's no surprise that China has the world's largest army, with around two million members. China wants the capability to defend itself from foreign aggressors. Maintaining control also means stemming opposition, so internal security is high.

CLOSE RELATIONSHIP

China's first communist leaders owed their positions to military success during the civil war, so the CPC has had strong links with the People's Liberation Army (PLA). They have a mutually beneficial relationship – the Party's legitimacy depends on the PLA's support, and the PLA would be lost without the Party's financial support.

LOYAL MEMBERS

The PLA is made up of the country's army, navy and air force. Established in the 1920s as the military arm of the CPC, it was originally called the Red Army. Today, officers are Party members. To ensure loyalty, each military unit has a political officer answerable to the Party. As part of their military training, recruits are also required to read CPC speeches.

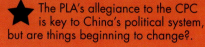

★ The PLA's allegiance to the CPC is key to China's political system, but are things beginning to change?.

RECENT REFORMS

The PLA has undergone a campaign of intense modernisation. Since the 1980s, reforms have reduced the force by half. The aim is to transform the PLA from a large ground force to a smaller, high-tech military, and to give a greater role to the navy to expand China's global influence. Concentrating on quality over quantity has brought better training, weapons and pay.

As chairman of the Central Military Commission, Xi Jinping also takes charge of the People's Armed Police (PAP), seen here guarding Mao Zedong's tomb.

CHANGING TIMES

There has been speculation that the relationship between the Party and the PLA is beginning to change. There is currently no PLA representative on the Politburo Standing Committee, for example, and as new commander-in-chief of the PLA Joint Battle Command, some say Xi Jinping runs the PLA himself. Others argue the PLA is moving away from Party loyalties, preferring to focus on national interests than internal security. Whatever the reality, citizens believe a strong CPC and powerful PLA are the only ways to prevent another 'Century of Humiliation'.

'Strengthening the Party's leadership in the army is necessary for making China and its army powerful.'

Xi Jinping, speaking to PLA leaders, 2018

★ In 2019, Xi increased the defence budget as part of plans to create a world-class military, developing new stealth fighters (left), aircraft carriers and missiles.

WHAT ABOUT THE ECONOMY?

China's economy has grown rapidly in recent decades, averaging 9.5 per cent growth annually between 1989 and 2019. As the largest exporter and second largest importer of goods, China has great influence on the global economic stage. But a slowing market is forcing China to rethink its economic strategy.

AMBITIOUS GOALS

In the past, Chinese leaders have had to choose between fast political reform and slow economic growth, or slow reform and fast growth. But analysts claim recent decades have shown the CPC attempting both – reforming the economy while strengthening Party control. With the export market stagnating, China needs to move towards a consumption-based economy (technology and services), while keeping a stable job market.

KEEPING CONTROL

Party officials have direct access to those running China's largest state companies, using designated 'red phones' that link them. State companies also have CPC committees to uphold Party values, and these have been introduced to private and foreign-invested companies, too. Most firms cooperate because they want a stake in China's growing market.

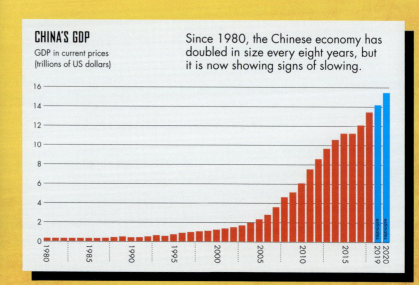

CHINA'S GDP

GDP in current prices (trillions of US dollars)

Since 1980, the Chinese economy has doubled in size every eight years, but it is now showing signs of slowing.

POWERFUL INFLUENCES

Successful entrepreneurs also hold great sway. Jack Ma (right), founder of online shopping giant Alibaba, was China's richest man before he retired in 2018, and secured one-to-one meetings with US presidents Barack Obama and Donald Trump. Ma Huateng, founder of WeChat, has great power within the technology sector, as does Sun Yafang, chairwoman of Huawei (see page 37). But these people are closely linked with the CPC. Following a Party investigation in 2017, billionaire property tycoon Wang Jianlin reduced his company's international ambitions. Xi Jinping's anti-corruption drive has made it harder for entrepreneurs to buy political influence. Whatever someone's position, keeping on side with the authorities is key.

★ BELT AND ROAD INITIATIVE (BRI)

In 2013, Xi Jinping proposed an ambitious project called the Belt and Road Initiative (BRI). Inspired by the ancient Silk Road trade route, it seeks to boost trade and economic growth by connecting Asia, Africa and Europe via land and sea networks, at a cost of around US$4 trillion. Over 70 countries have signed up to the project so far, accounting for about a third of the world's trade. This map shows the links between some key cities along the route.

WHAT INFLUENCE DOES CHINA HAVE?

Today, what happens in China has a direct impact on the rest of the world. China's elevated position has given it an expanded role in global governance. China has also risen to become an economic competitor and, more significantly, a global leader in emerging markets such as technology.

TRADING PARTNERS

In trade, too, China is showing dominance and its allies are growing. Australia, for example, provides China with valuable natural resources, while China has invested heavily in Australian mining. Some analysts believe China has kept Australia out of recession for over 25 years. Australia is a traditional ally of the USA, so as its relationship with China deepens, economic forecasters say that Australia may have to choose between them.

GLOBAL VOICE

China now has a firm footing on the world stage. Having joined the United Nations (UN) in 1971, the International Monetary Fund and World Bank in 1980 and the World Trade Organization in 2001, it is sitting comfortably among the world's greats. Significantly, China is one of five nations to have the power of a veto in the UN, which gives it control over UN decisions and enables it to block actions put forward by the international community.

The five permanent members of the UN – the UK, Russia, USA, China and France – have the power of a veto. The People's Republic of China has used it 13 times.

SHIFTING BALANCE

In 2009, China surpassed the USA as Africa's largest trading partner. Developing countries have traditionally been linked to Western nations for trade and aid agreements. But China is offering an alternative solution for economic growth – by strengthening trade ties and financing infrastructure projects. Some commentators say these investments are exploitative, however, saddling developing countries with debt and causing environmental degradation. China has also been accused of changing global trade rules, by relaxing environmental regulations and intellectual property rights.

★ In 2019, China's status rose further as the first country to land a lunar probe on the 'dark side' of the Moon – shown here as an artist's impression.

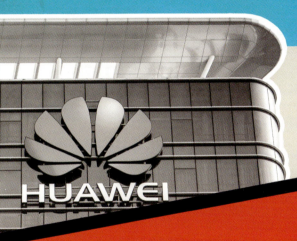

Huawei is now the world's largest telecom equipment supplier and the second largest smartphone maker (after Samsung).

★ HUAWEI

The rapid rise of Chinese technology company Huawei has raised suspicions in the West. There have been claims that the company's links with the Chinese government pose national security risks. Concerns intensified with the development of 5G wireless networks (which have faster download speeds). Some nations, such as the USA and Australia, have banned Huawei from providing equipment for their 5G networks. Although national security is at the heart of the matter, market protection is also at stake. Could this be the start of a 'digital iron curtain', as countries opt for or against Huawei technology?

WHAT ABOUT GLOBAL INFLUENCES?

While China is building bridges with the world (both real and metaphorical), the USA is putting up walls. They are both doing this to protect the particular circumstances of their nations. But this change in US policy is opening doors for China – and China won't wait to be invited in.

MUSCLING IN

As the world's reliance on oil wanes, US presence in the Middle East is dwindling. China still needs oil, however, and access to new markets to increase its influence. It's no coincidence that trade between China and Saudi Arabia rose by 32 per cent in 2018, for example, or that King Salman visited China before the USA in 2019. But China has to tread carefully, since it also has ties with Saudi Arabia's foe, Iran.

OLD LOYALTIES

Other relations are based on more than economic gain. North Korea, for example, is a useful buffer between China and US-backed South Korea. Although North Korea's nuclear testing program has caused a strain in recent years, China is its biggest trading partner and a source of aid and fuel. China wants to avoid regime collapse in North Korea, which could cause a flood of refugees or reunification with South Korea, leading to a US ally on its border.

★ With plentiful oil and emerging markets, China is keen to develop its relationship with the Middle East.

TRADE WAR

In 2018, the USA began a trade war with China. It accused China of stealing technology from US companies and hit back by increasing import tariffs on Chinese goods, making them more expensive to buy. China retaliated in the same manner. But the world's two largest economies are deeply connected. Many US products such as Apple devices, for example, are now made in China, and the trade war impacted their sales.

CHANGES OF ALLEGIANCE

US trade tariffs have forced China to find alternative suppliers of agricultural products such as soya beans from Russia. Similarly, anti-Russian sanctions from the West led Russia to grant Chinese investors access to its energy sector. A new 3,000 km gas pipeline from Russia to China will supply 38 billion cubic metres of natural gas annually, as part of a 30-year agreement. In 2019, China and Russia signed more than US$20 billion worth of trade deals to strengthen economic ties between them.

'As we open our eyes to look at the world, we are faced with huge changes, changes not seen in 100 years.'

Xi Jinping,
New Year message,
December 2018

★ China Ocean Shipping Company (COSCO) is one of the world's largest shipping operators, but US tariffs are affecting trade.

INDUSTRIAL CONSEQUENCES

After years of population growth and rapid industrialisation, China has paid a heavy price environmentally. Increased air and water pollution, soil erosion and depleted water resources are just some of the issues the country faces. Can China reduce its ecological footprint, without disrupting an already slowing economy?

A recent report revealed that over one million people die prematurely in China every year due to the effects of air pollution.

'We must establish and practise the philosophy that lucid waters and lush mountains are invaluable assets... build a beautiful China, create a good production and living environment for the people, and contribute to global ecological safety.'

Xi Jinping, outlining the principles of Xi Jinping Thought, 2017

RECTIFYING ITS WAYS

The government has invested heavily in environmental reform and regulation. China was once home to the world's most polluted cities, but by 2015, none were in the top 20. China has reduced its dependence on coal and is now considered a global leader in renewable energy. It aims to source a fifth of its energy from renewable sources by 2030, and has started collecting an environmental tax to fund initiatives. The CPC has also strengthened environmental regulations, placing penalties on those who falsify records or dispose of waste incorrectly.

SOCIAL CHANGE

China's growing middle class has become more attuned to environmental issues, particularly those affecting health, such as the impact of pollution on food safety. The government needs to address these concerns to maintain political stability. Wealthier lifestyles are also adding to the crisis – with increased energy use and the growth of factory farming of beef and pork, for example.

INTERNATIONAL COOPERATION

Despite the gravity of the situation, the environmental crisis has also opened doors for China. China wants to be seen as a responsible member of the global community, and agreed to sign the Paris Climate Agreement in 2016. The country has also found new foreign markets keen to use its low-cost renewable energy products such as solar panels. Xi Jinping talks about building a beautiful China, through environmental protection and 'green' investments. Some commentators believe China has the potential to be the world's environmental saviour – its ultimate trump card.

★ China has committed to cut carbon dioxide emissions to less than half what they were in 2005 by 2030.

★ China uses more electricity than any country, but is also the biggest producer of clean solar energy.

HOW DOES XI JINPING WANT TO GOVERN?

In a throwback to the time of Deng Xiaoping, Xi's ideals are described as 'socialism with Chinese characteristics for a new era'. Xi wants to build a strong and wealthy China, creating sustainable economic growth, reducing inequalities in wealth, stamping out corruption, tackling pollution and making China a great military power.

PARTY POLITICS

Xi has turned his back on collective leadership, preferring to centralise his authority. In 2018, the NPC made a constitutional amendment to abolish two-term limits, meaning Xi could effectively govern for life. Xi has become head of a number of 'task forces', with greater power to advance policies. His anti-corruption drive has helped allies rise through the ranks. A lengthy rule could bring stability during times of change, but commentators have raised concerns about dictatorial power.

★ Xi is seen as China's most influential leader since Mao Zedong. Here he meets workers at China National Petroleum Corporation.

In 2017, 'Xi Jinping Thought' was written into China's constitution. Xi proposed the 'Chinese Dream', which sees the nation become a global leader in areas such as science, diplomacy and culture. He also talks of two centenary goals – creating a 'moderately well-off society' by 2021 and a 'democratic, civilised, harmonious and modern socialist country' by 2049.

WORLD TRADE

Xi wants economic growth to keep people in jobs, and wages rising. His 'let's all win' attitude to world trade has encouraged developing nations, too. He insists he's not seeking world dominance, but analysts suggest dominance may come to China regardless. In 2015, China began the 'Made in China 2025' initiative, to move China from manufacturing cheap goods to more high-tech products. The aim is to be a global leader in industries such as aerospace, robotics, electric vehicles and high-tech medical equipment.

Vietnam, the Philippines, Brunei, Malaysia and Taiwan lay claim to the Spratly and Paracel islands, but China says it has owned the region since ancient times. Non-claimants want the sea kept free for trade.

FOREIGN POLICY

Xi would also like to see China regaining lost lands. Recent expansion in the South China Sea, for example, has been seen as a sign of territorial ambition. For the past decade, China has built artificial islands in the region, with military reinforcement to defend its claim. This issue is about more than just prestige and power. Not only is this one of the world's most valuable trading routes, the region is also host to vital fishing areas and important gas and oil reserves.

WHAT LIES AHEAD?

No country has changed as greatly as China in the past 50 years. Once a largely agricultural society damaged by the memories of foreign invasion, China has re-emerged as a vibrant leader on the world stage. Many experts believe the twenty-first century will belong to China. There's no doubt the once sleeping giant is one to watch.

SOCIAL CARE

As China's population ages (see page 14), pensions and social care will become a dominant issue. To redress China's demographic problems, families are being urged to have at least two children – but many still choose to have just one. Female career progression, the costs of living and child rearing and the competitive nature of education have all contributed to a culture of small families.

FOREIGN AFFAIRS

Today, the shifting international landscape is in China's favour. The controversial US presidential election and UK Brexit vote in 2016 have also been used to convey the weaknesses of democracy. China's system isn't safe – over-concentration of power brings the risk of rebellion (internally or globally), but China is gaining support from those keen to cash in on its success, even at the expense of human rights.

★ China opened the longest sea bridge in 2018, linking Hong Kong, Macao and Zhuhai, at a cost of US$20 billion.

WORKING TOGETHER

Since the nineteenth century, a few key states have vied for global dominance. The USA has been on top for some time, but China is now proving a worthy contender. Will China seek dominance or will it work towards a more harmonious future, where states come together for the common good, instead of competing? With environmental issues becoming a matter of urgency, perhaps this is the time to work towards what Xi calls a 'shared future'.

'The Chinese Dream is a dream about history, the present, and the future. It is a dream of our generation, but even more so a dream of the younger generations.'

Xi Jinping, CPC 19th National Congress, 2017

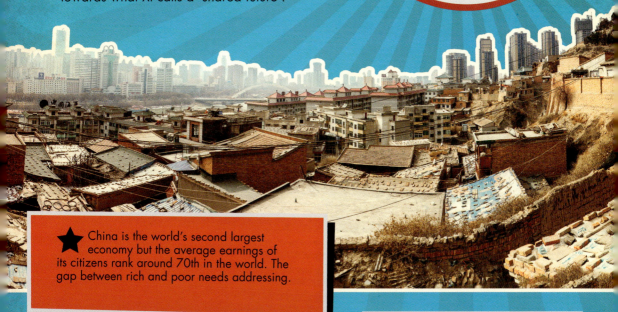

★ China is the world's second largest economy but the average earnings of its citizens rank around 70th in the world. The gap between rich and poor needs addressing.

LAST WORD

As we look back at China's chequered history, the choices leaders made were suited to the particular needs of the time. Some initiatives worked – others failed but led to a different tack. Some analysts have suggested a cyclical pattern of centralised rule versus collective leadership. Yet for all its strengths and weaknesses, China's national interests have to be addressed within a global context – and only time will tell what the future holds.

China's children are increasingly educated and many young people now travel abroad. Can the Party withstand the growing power of future generations?

GLOSSARY

Arab Spring
A series of anti-government protests that spread across the Middle East in 2011.

autonomous region
A region that is allowed to control its own affairs.

capitalism
A system of government in which property is privately owned and goods are traded competitively.

communism
A system of government in which everything is owned by the community. Everyone gives according to their abilities and takes according to their needs.

Communist Youth League
A youth movement run by the CPC for those aged 14–28.

constitution
A set of written principles of the way a country is governed and the rights of its citizens.

Cultural Revolution
A socio-political movement (1966–76) led by China's Mao Zedong, to reinstate communist values by influencing people's attitudes and behaviour.

demographic
The structure of a population.

dissident
A person who publicly disagrees with their government's policies.

factory farming
An intensive method of farming used to increase production, at the expense of the environment.

Falun Gong
A spiritual movement founded in 1992. It quickly grew in China until it was banned there in 1999.

free trade
International trade in which goods and services are not subjected to tariffs, quotas, subsidies or other restrictions.

Great Leap Forward
An economic and social campaign (1958–61) led by Mao Zedong, to rapidly increase China's economy.

gross domestic product (GDP)
The monetary value of a country's goods and services; it is used as a general measure of the state of the economy.

inflation
A rise in the general cost of goods, so money is worth less.

infrastructure
The systems and services (such as transport and power supplies) that help a country to work effectively.

intellectual property rights
Rights such as patents, trademarks and copyright that allow the holder sole use of an item or idea for a given time without the risk of competition.

Manchuria
A region of north-eastern China, the ownership of which has been disputed throughout history between China, Russia and Japan.

open market
A free-trade market in which prices are based on competition, not controlled by the government.

Paris Climate Agreement
An international agreement signed in 2016 to help combat climate change.

princeling
The heir of a powerful Chinese political family, advantaged by social status.

Red Guards
A student-led movement, guided by Mao Zedong during the Cultural Revolution. The group wore military-style clothing and red armbands.

sanctions
Penalties for disobeying an international law or agreement; such as putting limits on trade.

socialism
A system of government in which the community owns the means of production. Citizens receive according to their ability and needs. Often regarded as a stage between communism and capitalism.

Special Economic Zone (SEZ)
An area with different business and trade laws (such as tax incentives), designed to attract foreign investment.

supply chain
The processes involved in the creation and sale of a product.

Taiwan
A Chinese island, home to the Republic of China since 1949. Today, Taiwan is an independent democratic nation, but China claims control over it.

World Trade Organization
An international organisation that deals with the rules of trade between nations.

FURTHER INFORMATION

BOOKS

China (Journey Through), Liz Gogerly and Rob Hunt, Franklin Watts, 2018

Communism (Systems of Government), Sean Connolly, Franklin Watts, 2017

China and Beijing (Developing World), Philip Steele, Franklin Watts, 2016

China: the new superpower? (World Issues), Antony Mason, Franklin Watts, 2005

China (Eyewitness), Poppy Sebag-Montefiore, DK Publishing, 2007

All About Politics (Big Questions), Andrew Marr, DK Publishing, 2016

WEBSITES

China country profile
www.bbc.co.uk/news/world-asia-pacific-13017877

A profile of China's current president, Xi Jinping
www.bbc.co.uk/news/world-asia-pacific-11551399

An in-depth look at China's system of government
news.bbc.co.uk/1/shared/spl/hi/in_depth/china_politics/government/html/1.stm

A timeline of key events in Chinese history
www.bbc.co.uk/news/world-asia-pacific-13017882

The official website of the Chinese government
www.gov.cn/english

Fascinating facts about China, its government and its people
www.china-family-adventure.com/china-facts.html

INDEX

Africa 35, 37

agriculture 6, 7, 8, 9, 10, 11, 14, 39, 44

aid 37, 38

Arab Spring 22

Australia 36

autonomous regions 4, 30

balance of power 5, 37

Beijing 4, 11, 13, 28, 31

Belt and Road Initiative (BRI) 35

Bo Xilai 24, 25

border 4, 5, 26, 32, 38

Central Military Commission 12, 16, 17, 29, 33

'Century of Humiliation' 5, 9, 15, 33

Chiang Kai-shek 8

Chinese Civil War 8, 32

communism 5, 6–7, 8–9, 10–11, 16

Communist Party of China (CPC) 8, 9, 10, 11, 12, 14, 16, 17, 20–21, 22–23, 24–25, 26, 27, 28, 29, 30, 31, 32, 33, 34, 35, 40, 45

Communist Youth League (CYL) 18, 31

constitution 28, 42, 43

corruption 11, 14, 24–25, 35, 42

Cultural Revolution 9

Deng Xiaoping 10–11, 12, 15, 29, 42

economy 5, 9, 10, 11, 12, 13, 14, 15, 16, 18, 19, 22, 24, 29, 31, 34–35, 37, 38, 39, 40, 42, 43, 45

education 4, 7, 21, 31, 44, 45

emperors 5, 8

Engels, Friedrich 7

entrepreneurs 31, 35

environment 13, 14, 15, 19, 24, 37, 40–41, 42, 45

ethnic groups 4, 26, 30

Falun Gong 27

France 5, 13, 36

Germany 5, 13, 19

Great Leap Forward 9

healthcare 4

Hong Kong 4, 12, 15, 30, 44

Hu Jintao 12, 13, 14, 17, 18, 19, 22

Huawei 35, 37

human rights 24, 26–27, 44

industrialisation 5, 8, 9, 14, 40

industry 6, 8, 11, 43

inequality 6, 7, 14, 42, 45

infrastructure 13, 35, 37

International Monetary Fund 36

internet 21, 22–23, 27

Japan 5, 8, 10, 13

Jiang Zemin 12, 14

jobs 4, 5, 7, 9, 10, 14, 20, 34, 43

Kuomintang (KMT) 8

Li Keqiang 18–19, 29

Liu Xiaobo 27

local government 30–31

Macao 4, 30, 44

Manchuria 8

Mao Zedong 8–9, 10, 15, 17, 33, 42

Marx, Karl 7

media 21, 23

Middle East 22, 38

migration 14, 15

military 8, 11, 12, 16, 17, 19, 21, 28, 29, 32–33, 42, 43

National Party Congress 28, 31, 45

National People's Congress (NPC) 20, 28, 29, 42

North Korea 4, 20, 38

Olympics 13

one-child policy 10, 14, 15, 21, 26, 30, 44

Paris Climate Agreement 41

People's Liberation Army (PLA) (see military)

People's Republic of China 8, 36

Politburo 17, 19, 24, 25, 28, 29, 33

population 4, 5, 10, 14, 15, 16, 19, 20, 22, 26, 30, 40, 44

provinces 18, 19, 30, 31

religion 7, 27

Republic of China 8

Russia 4, 5, 6, 16, 36, 39

sanctions 39

Saudi Arabia 38

Second World War 8

Shanghai 4, 12, 15, 17, 31

Shenzhen 4, 13

social credit system 27

social media 23, 35

socialism 10, 42, 43

South China Sea 15, 43

Soviet Union 10

Special Economic Zones (SEZs) 11, 13

State Council 18, 19, 29

Taiwan 4, 8, 15, 27, 30, 43

technology 10, 11, 13, 33, 34, 35, 36, 37, 39, 43

Tiananmen Square 11, 12, 29

Tibet 4, 15, 26

trade 12, 13, 19, 34, 35, 36, 37, 38, 39, 41, 43

UK 13, 36, 44

United Nations (UN) 36

USA 4, 5, 10, 12, 26, 35, 36, 37, 38, 39, 44, 45

welfare 4, 7, 12, 14, 19, 44

women 9, 15, 28, 31

World Bank 36

World Trade Organization 12, 36

Xi Jinping 14, 16–17, 19, 20, 22, 24, 25, 26, 28, 29, 31, 33, 35, 39, 40, 41, 42–43, 45

Xinjiang 4, 15, 26, 27

Zhou Yongkang 25

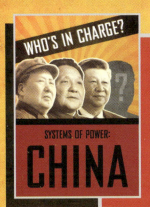

CHINA

WHAT makes China unique?
WHAT is communism?
HOW did China's communism change?
WHAT are today's key challenges?
WHO is Xi Jinping?
WHO is Li Keqiang?
WHAT is a one-party state?
WHAT about human rights?

HOW does the government work?
WHY is the army important?
WHAT about the economy?
WHAT influence does China have?
WHAT about global influences?
HOW does Xi Jinping want to govern?
WHAT lies ahead?

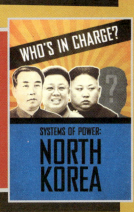

NORTH KOREA

WHAT makes North Korea unique?
WHEN was North Korea founded?
WHAT is communism?
WHO are the Kim family?
WHAT is a one-party state?
HOW does the government work?
WHAT is daily life like?

WHAT about human rights?
WHAT about nuclear weapons?
HOW are neighbouring relations?
WHAT about the rest of the world?
WHY is the army important?
WHAT about the economy?
WHAT lies ahead?

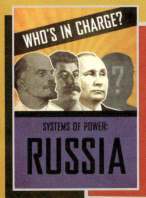

RUSSIA

WHAT makes Russia unique?
WHAT political system does Russia have?
HOW was Russia governed in the past?
WHY did communism end?
HOW is the government structured?
WHO is Vladimir Putin?
WHO is Dmitry Medvedev?
WHAT are today's key challenges?

WHY are environmental issues important?
WHAT resources does Russia have?
WHAT about the economy?
WHAT is Russia's nuclear status?
WHAT about human rights?
HOW does Russia exert a global influence?
WHAT are Russia's international relations like?
WHAT lies ahead?

SAUDI ARABIA

WHAT makes Saudi Arabia unique?
WHO are the Sa'ud family?
WHO is King Salman?
WHO is Mohammed bin Salman?
WHAT is an absolute monarchy?
HOW is the government structured?
WHAT is Sharia law?

WHAT are today's key challenges?
WHAT about human rights?
WHAT about the economy?
WHY is the military important?
WHAT influence does Saudi Arabia have?
WHAT are its global relations like?
WHAT lies ahead?

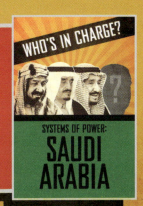

Published in Great Britain in MMXVII by
Book House, an imprint of
The Salariya Book Company Ltd
25 Marlborough Place, Brighton BN1 1UB
www.salariya.com

ISBN: 978-1-910706-68-8

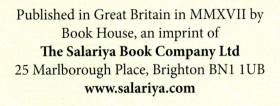

A CIP catalogue record for this book is available
from the British Library.

Printed and bound in China.